WIX WEBSITE SIMPLIFIED

The Complete Guide to Create Build
Stunning and Professional Websites
Optimized for SEO & Get Your
Business Online Faster and Easier

Andrew G. Willard

CONTENTS

FOREWORD

The individual standing next to you will most likely tell you that they created their first website using Wix if you ask them what it is. However, that is not the entire tale. Yes, Wix is a fantastic website builder for both experts in web design and those just learning how to develop websites, but it's much more than that. Trust me *WIX Website Simplified: The Complete Guide to Create Build Stunning and Professional Websites Optimized for SEO & Get Your Business Online Faster and Easier* will do justice to that, but before we go deep, it is necessary to understand that in the contemporary time coupled with the rapidly evolving digital landscape, having an online presence is no longer a luxury but a necessity. Whether you're a small business owner, entrepreneur, or an individual seeking to share your unique story with the world, a website is your gateway to reaching a broader audience and establishing a strong digital footprint.

However, the process of creating a website can often seem intimidating, especially for those without prior technical expertise. This is where Wix, a powerful and user-friendly website builder, comes into play. With its intuitive interface and vast array of features, Wix empowers anyone to create stunning websites with ease, regardless of their technical background.

One of the key strengths of this guide is its emphasis on practicality. Rather than overwhelming you with technical jargon, it focuses on providing real-world examples and practical tips that you can apply immediately. You'll learn how to create a mobile-friendly design, optimize your site for search engines, integrate e-commerce functionality, and much more – all while ensuring that your website accurately represents your brand or personal vision. But this book is not just about creating a website; it's also about empowering you to take control of your online presence. You'll gain valuable insights into best practices for website maintenance, analytics, and ongoing optimization, ensuring that your site remains relevant and engaging for your audience.

INTRODUCTION

Wix is a robust website builder that doesn't require any coding knowledge. It can be used to create anything from a basic personal blog to a sophisticated enterprise-level center for your online business. It comes with built-in tools for scheduling, branding, marketing, eCommerce, and more. An established player in the internet market, Wix has a history of being a pioneer in web design and an early user of cutting-edge innovations, such as AI website building.

Whether you're a small business owner seeking to expand your reach, an entrepreneur looking to showcase your products or services, or an individual with a unique story to share, a well-designed website can be a game-changer, having an online presence is crucial for businesses and individuals alike especially in the contemporary time. However, the process of creating a website can often seem daunting, especially for those without prior technical expertise. This is where Wix, a powerful and user-friendly website builder, comes in. With its intuitive interface and vast array of features, Wix empowers anyone to create stunning websites with ease, regardless of their technical background.

One of the key strengths of *WIX Website Simplified: The Complete Guide to Create Build Stunning and Professional Websites Optimized for SEO & Get Your Business Online Faster and Easier* is its emphasis on practicality. Rather than overwhelming you with technical jargon, it focuses on providing real-world examples and practical tips that you can apply immediately. You'll learn how to create a mobile-friendly design, optimize your site for search engines, integrate e-commerce functionality, and much more – all while ensuring that your website accurately represents your brand or personal vision.

But this book is not just about creating a website; it's also about empowering you to take control of your online presence. You'll gain valuable insights into best practices for website maintenance, analytics, and ongoing optimization, ensuring that your site remains relevant and engaging for your audience. Whether you're a complete beginner or have some experience with website building, this guide will serve as a valuable resource, guiding you through the process of creating a website that truly represents you or your business. By the time you've completed this book, you'll not only have a stunning website but also a newfound confidence in your ability to navigate the digital world and create an online presence that stands out from the crowd.

Open the pages of this book, and let your website dreams come to life with the power of Wix and the guidance of *WIX Website Simplified: The Complete Guide to Create Build Stunning and Professional Websites Optimized for SEO & Get Your Business Online Faster and Easier.*

WIX Website Simplified

The Complete Guide to Create Build Stunning and
Professional Websites Optimized for SEO & Get
Your Business Online Faster and Easier.

By: Andrew G. Willard

CHAPTER ONE

GETTING STARTED WITH WIX

Introduction To Wix

Wix is a powerful and user-friendly website builder that allows anyone, regardless of technical expertise, to create professional-looking websites with ease. It offers a vast array of features, templates, and design elements that empower users to bring their online presence to life without needing to know complex coding languages. Wix is a robust website builder that doesn't require any coding knowledge. It can be used to create anything from a basic personal blog to a sophisticated enterprise-level center for your online business. It comes with built-in tools for scheduling, branding, marketing, eCommerce, etc.

With Wix, you can create websites for various purposes, such as personal portfolios, small business websites, online stores, blogs, and more. The platform's intuitive interface and drag-and-drop functionality make it a breeze to customize your website's layout, add content, and integrate various functionalities.

Benefits Of Using Wix

1. **No Coding Required**: Wix eliminates the need for coding expertise, making website creation accessible to everyone, regardless of their technical background.

2. **Responsive Design**: Wix websites are automatically optimized for various devices, ensuring a seamless browsing experience across desktops, tablets, and smartphones.

3. **Extensive Design Options**: With hundreds of professionally designed templates and an extensive library of design elements, you can create a unique and visually appealing website that reflects your brand.

4. **Easy Content Management**: Adding and updating content on your Wix website is straightforward, thanks to the user-friendly content management system (CMS).

5. **E-Commerce Capabilities**: Wix offers robust e-commerce features, allowing you to set up an online store, manage inventory, and process payments securely.

6. **SEO Tools**: Wix provides built-in search engine optimization (SEO) tools to help improve your website's visibility and ranking in search engine results.

7. **Mobile App**: The Wix mobile app enables you to manage and update your website on-the-go, ensuring your online presence is always up-to-date.

Creating A Wix Account

Getting started with Wix is a straightforward process. Simply visit the Wix website (www.wix.com) and follow these steps:

1. Click on the "Get Started" button to begin creating your account.
2. Choose whether you want to create a website for personal or business purposes.
3. Provide your email address and create a secure password.
4. Optionally, you can sign up using your existing Google or Facebook account for faster registration.
5. Complete any additional information required, such as your name and website preferences.
6. Agree to the terms of service and privacy policy.
7. Click "Create Account" to finalize the registration process.

Once your account is created, you'll be redirected to the Wix Editor, where you can start building your website immediately.

Understanding The Wix Interface

Wix's user interface is designed to be intuitive and user-friendly, making it easy for beginners to navigate and explore its features. Let's take a closer look at the main components:

Dashboard Overview

The Wix Dashboard is your central hub for managing your website(s) and account settings. Here, you can:

- Access and edit your existing websites
- Create new websites
- Manage your account details and billing information
- Access the Wix App Market to explore and install additional features and integrations
- View and manage your website's analytics, SEO settings, and marketing tools
- Access support resources, tutorials, and the Wix community

Site Manager

The Site Manager is where you'll spend most of your time when working on your website. It provides a comprehensive set of tools and features to customize and manage your website's content, design, and functionality. Here, you can:

- Edit and customize your website's pages and layout
- Add, modify, and organize your website's content (text, images, videos, etc.)
- Manage your website's navigation and menus
- Integrate third-party applications and services
- Customize your website's design and styling

- Configure advanced settings, such as SEO, analytics, and domain management

Editor Tools

Within the Site Manager, you'll find the Editor Tools panel, which provides easy access to various editing tools and features. These tools allow you to:

- Add and customize design elements (e.g., text boxes, images, shapes, galleries, videos)
- Adjust the layout and positioning of elements on your pages
- Modify element styles (e.g., colors, fonts, backgrounds)
- Preview your website's appearance on different devices (desktop, tablet, mobile)
- Undo and redo changes
- Access advanced design settings and options

App Market

The Wix App Market is a vast library of third-party applications, integrations, and add-ons that can enhance your website's functionality and capabilities. From e-commerce solutions to social media integrations, form builders, and marketing tools, the App Market offers a wide range of options to customize your website according to your specific needs.

In the next section, we'll dive deeper into the process of creating a new website using Wix, exploring various design elements and advanced features to help you build a professional-looking online presence.

CHAPTER TWO

DESIGNING YOUR WEBSITE

Choosing A Template Or Theme

Exploring Template Options

Wix offers a vast collection of professionally designed templates to kickstart your website creation process. These templates are organized into various categories, such as business, portfolio, online store, and more, making it easier to find a suitable starting point for your specific needs. Take the time to browse through the available options, paying attention to the layout, color schemes, and overall aesthetics. Keep in mind that these templates are fully customizable, so you can tailor them to match your brand identity and vision.

Customizing Templates

Once you've selected a template that aligns with your goals, you can begin customizing it to suit your preferences. Wix's intuitive editor allows you to make modifications with ease. You can rearrange elements, change colors, swap images, and adjust typography to create a unique look and feel. Don't be afraid to experiment and make the template your own – the flexibility of Wix's platform empowers you to craft a website that truly represents your brand.

Using Custom Code

For those with coding expertise or specific design requirements, Wix offers the ability to incorporate custom HTML, CSS, and JavaScript code into your website. This advanced feature enables you to enhance functionality, integrate third-party tools, and achieve a truly unique and tailored online presence. However, it's important to exercise caution when working with custom code to ensure compatibility and maintain the overall integrity of your website.

Customizing The Design

Working with Wix Editor

The Wix Editor is the heart of the website design process. This powerful tool provides a user-friendly interface where you can drag and drop various elements onto your website canvas. From text boxes and images to buttons and forms, the Editor offers a wide range of customizable components to bring your vision to life. Additionally, you can access advanced settings and options for each element, allowing for precise control over positioning, styling, and behavior.

Adjusting Layout and Structure

Creating an organized and visually appealing layout is

crucial for an effective website design. Wix allows you to easily manipulate the structure of your pages by adding or removing sections, adjusting column widths, and aligning elements. You can also utilize grid systems and predefined layouts to maintain consistency and ensure a professional appearance throughout your website.

Working with Colors and Fonts

Color Schemes

Color plays a significant role in setting the tone and conveying the personality of your brand. Wix provides a comprehensive color palette, allowing you to choose from a wide range of pre-defined color schemes or create your own custom combinations. Experiment with different hues, shades, and tints to find the perfect palette that resonates with your target audience and aligns with your branding.

Typography

Typography is another essential element that contributes to the overall aesthetic and readability of your website. Wix offers a vast selection of font families, weights, and styles, empowering you to create visually appealing and legible text elements. Explore different typefaces and pairing combinations to establish a unique typographic hierarchy that enhances the user experience and reinforces your brand identity.

Adding Multimedia Elements

Images and Graphics

Visuals are powerful tools for capturing attention and communicating your message effectively. Wix allows you to easily upload and incorporate high-quality images and graphics onto your website. You can resize, crop, and apply various effects to these visual elements, ensuring they seamlessly integrate with your overall design. Additionally, Wix provides access to a vast library of stock images, icons, and illustrations, allowing you to enhance your website's visual appeal without the need for costly image resources.

Videos

Video content has become increasingly popular and engaging for website visitors. Wix simplifies the process of embedding videos from various sources, such as YouTube, Vimeo, or your own library. You can customize the video player's appearance, set autoplay options, and even create video galleries or playlists to showcase multiple videos in a visually appealing manner.

Audio

Adding audio elements to your website can create an immersive and engaging experience for your visitors. Wix allows you to easily upload and embed audio files, such as background music, podcasts, or sound effects. You can control the playback settings, including looping and autoplay, to ensure a seamless audio experience throughout your website.

Creating A Mobile-Friendly Design

Responsive Design Principles

It's essential to ensure that your website is optimized for various screen sizes and devices. Wix embraces responsive design principles, automatically adjusting the layout and elements of your website to provide an optimal viewing experience on desktop computers, tablets, and smartphones. This feature ensures that your content is accessible and user-friendly, regardless of the device used to access your website.

Mobile Editor

Wix takes mobile-friendliness a step further by offering a dedicated Mobile Editor. This tool allows you to preview and customize the appearance of your website specifically for mobile devices. You can rearrange elements, adjust font sizes, and fine-tune the layout to ensure a seamless and intuitive experience for your mobile visitors.

Testing on Different Devices

While Wix's responsive design features are robust, it's always a good practice to test your website on various devices and screen sizes. Wix provides a device simulation tool that emulates different viewports, allowing you to identify and address any potential issues or inconsistencies before publishing your website to the public.

By following these guidelines and leveraging the powerful design tools provided by Wix, you can create a visually stunning, functional, and mobile-friendly website that effectively represents your brand and captivates your target audience.

CHAPTER THREE

BUILDING YOUR WEBSITE
CONTENT

Adding And Editing Pages

Creating New Pages

Building a website with Wix is a straightforward process that allows you to create professional-looking pages without extensive coding knowledge. To begin, you'll need to create new pages that will serve as the foundation for your website's content.

Adding a new page is as simple as clicking the "Add Page" button in the Wix editor. Once you've done that, you'll be presented with a variety of page layout options to choose from. These layouts are designed to cater to different types of content, such as a homepage, blog, portfolio, or online store.

Wix's page creation process is user-friendly, with drag-and-drop functionality that allows you to easily add and arrange elements on your page. You can customize the layout by resizing or repositioning sections, ensuring that your content is presented in the most visually appealing and organized manner.

Page Layouts

Wix offers a wide range of pre-designed page layouts to choose from, each tailored to specific purposes. For example, you might choose a layout optimized for showcasing products if you're building an online store, or a layout with prominent visuals if you're creating a photography portfolio.

These layouts are fully customizable, allowing you to modify them to suit your specific needs. You can add, remove, or rearrange sections, change the color scheme, and adjust the typography to match your branding and design preferences.

Page Navigation

Once you've created multiple pages, it's essential to ensure that your visitors can navigate between them seamlessly. Wix provides several options for page navigation, including a top menu, footer menu, or side navigation bar.

You can easily add links to your pages within these navigation elements, ensuring that your website's structure is intuitive and user-friendly. Wix also allows you to control the order in which your pages appear in the navigation menu, making it easy to organize your content in a logical and coherent manner.

Creating Navigation Menus

Menu Types

Wix offers a variety of menu types to choose from, each with its own unique style and functionality. Some of the most popular menu types include:

1. Horizontal Menu: This menu is typically placed at the top of the page and displays navigation links in a horizontal row.
2. Vertical Menu: As the name suggests, this menu displays navigation links in a vertical column, often used as a sidebar or side navigation.
3. Dropdown Menu: This menu type allows you to create multi-level navigation, with sub-menus appearing when the user hovers over or clicks on a main menu item.
4. Burger Menu: Also known as a hamburger menu, this compact menu style is ideal for mobile devices, condensing navigation links into a collapsible menu icon.

Menu Customization

Regardless of the menu type you choose, Wix provides ample customization options to ensure that your navigation menus complement the overall design and branding of your website. You can adjust the font, color, size, and spacing of menu items, as well as add icons or images to enhance the visual appeal.

Also, Wix allows you to control the behavior of your menus, such as whether sub-menus should appear on hover or click, and how they should animate when revealed. These customization options ensure that your navigation menus not only look great but also provide a smooth and intuitive user experience.

Working With Text And Images

Text Formatting

Presenting text in an engaging and visually appealing manner is crucial for capturing and retaining your visitors' attention. Wix provides a wide range of text formatting options, allowing you to customize the appearance of your content to suit your brand and design preferences. You can easily adjust the font family, size, color, and style (bold, italic, underline) of your text, ensuring that your content is both readable and aligned with your website's overall aesthetic. Wix also offers advanced formatting options, such as creating bulleted or numbered lists, adjusting line spacing, and adding indentation.

Image Optimization

Images play a vital role in enhancing the visual appeal of your website and conveying information more effectively. Wix makes it easy to upload and optimize images for your website, ensuring that they load quickly and maintain their quality. When uploading images, Wix automatically compresses them to reduce file size without compromising quality. This optimization process helps improve your website's loading speed, providing a better user experience for your visitors. Thus, Wix offers various image editing tools, allowing you to crop, rotate, and adjust the brightness, contrast, and saturation of your images directly within the editor. These tools ensure that your images look their best and complement the overall design of your website.

Incorporating Multimedia Elements

Embedding Videos

Video content has become increasingly popular on the web, as it offers an engaging and immersive way to convey information or showcase products and services. Wix makes it easy to embed videos from popular platforms like YouTube and Vimeo directly onto your website pages. To embed a video, simply copy and paste the video URL into the Wix editor, and the platform will automatically generate a video player that seamlessly integrates with your page design. You can customize the video player's appearance, such as adjusting its size, adding controls, or setting it to autoplay.

Adding Slideshows

Slideshows are an effective way to showcase multiple images or pieces of content in a visually appealing and interactive manner. Wix provides a user-friendly slideshow tool that allows you to create professional-looking slideshows with ease. You can add images, videos, or even entire website pages to your slideshow, and customize various settings such as transition effects, timing, and navigation controls. Slideshows can be embedded directly onto your website pages, making them a great way to showcase portfolios, product galleries, or highlight key features of your business.

Using Wix Apps And Widgets

App Market

Wix offers an extensive App Market, which is a repository of third-party applications and widgets that can be easily integrated into your website. These apps and widgets provide additional functionality and features, allowing you to enhance your website's capabilities without the need for complex coding. The App Market offers a wide range of options, including e-commerce solutions, contact forms, social media integrations, event calendars, and many more. You can browse and search for apps based on categories, popularity, or specific features, making it easy to find the tools you need to take your website to the next level.

Popular Apps and Widgets

Some of the most popular and widely used Wix apps and widgets include:

1. Wix Stores: This e-commerce app allows you to create an online store, manage inventory, and process payments directly from your Wix website.
2. Wix Blogs: This app enables you to create and manage a fully-featured blog, complete with categories, tags, comments, and social sharing options.
3. Wix Forms: With this app, you can create custom forms for various purposes, such as contact forms, surveys, or registration forms.
4. Social Media Feeds: These widgets allow you to seamlessly integrate your social media feeds onto your website, keeping your visitors up-to-date with your latest posts and updates.
5. Google Maps: This widget lets you embed interactive maps onto your website, making it easier for visitors to find your business location or navigate to specific destinations.

Customizing Apps

While Wix apps and widgets come with pre-designed templates and default settings, Wix also allows you to customize these elements to better fit your website's design and requirements. You can adjust the appearance of apps and widgets by changing colors, fonts, and layouts, ensuring that they blend seamlessly with your website's overall aesthetic. Additionally, many apps offer advanced settings and configurations, allowing you to tailor their functionality to meet your specific needs.

By leveraging the power of Wix's App Market and customization options, you can create a truly unique and feature-rich website that stands out from the competition.

CHAPTER FOUR

ADVANCED FEATURES

Integrating E-Commerce

Setting up an Online Store

Creating an online store using Wix is a straightforward process. The platform offers a user-friendly interface and a variety of tools to help you set up and manage your e-commerce business effectively. Start by selecting the 'Online Store' option from the Wix Editor, which will guide you through the process of customizing your store's layout, design, and functionality.

Begin by defining your product categories and subcategories, making it easier for customers to navigate and find what they're looking for. Next, add your products by providing detailed descriptions, high-quality images, pricing information, and inventory levels. Wix allows you to create product variations, such as different sizes, colors, or materials, ensuring that your customers have a wide range of options to choose from.

Payment Gateways

Integrating secure payment gateways is crucial for any online store. Wix offers seamless integration with popular payment processors, such as PayPal, Stripe, and Square, ensuring that your customers can make purchases with confidence. These payment gateways allow you to accept various payment methods, including credit cards, debit cards, and digital wallets. When setting up your payment gateway, ensure that you provide clear instructions and streamline the checkout process to minimize cart abandonment rates. Additionally, consider offering multiple payment options to cater to your customers' preferences and increase conversion rates.

Inventory Management

Effective inventory management is essential for running a successful online store. Wix provides robust inventory management tools that allow you to track stock levels, receive low-stock notifications, and manage product variants efficiently. You can also set up automatic stock updates, ensuring that your inventory levels are always accurate and up-to-date.

By leveraging Wix's inventory management features, you can streamline your operations, prevent overselling, and maintain excellent customer satisfaction levels by ensuring that products are available for purchase.

Search Engine Optimization (Seo)

On-Page SEO

On-page SEO refers to the optimization techniques you apply directly to your website's content and structure. Wix offers a range of features to help you improve your on-page SEO, including:

1. Title tags and meta descriptions: Customize these elements to accurately represent your website's content and include relevant keywords.
2. Header tags: Use heading tags (H1, H2, H3) to structure your content and make it easier for search engines to understand the hierarchy of information.
3. Image optimization: Provide descriptive alt text for images, which aids in accessibility and search engine indexing.
4. URL structure: Create user-friendly and keyword-rich URLs that reflect the content of each page.

Off-Page SEO

Off-page SEO focuses on activities outside of your website that can influence its search engine rankings. While Wix doesn't directly control off-page SEO, the platform provides tools and resources to help you optimize these factors:

1. Link building: Encourage high-quality websites to link back to your Wix site, as this can improve your website's authority and rankings.

2. Social media integration: Promote your content on social media platforms to increase visibility and potential backlinks.

3. Local SEO: If your business serves a specific geographic area, optimize your Wix site for local SEO by claiming your Google My Business listing and incorporating location-specific keywords.

Analytics And Tracking

Wix integrates with various analytics tools, including Google Analytics, to provide valuable insights into your website's performance. By tracking metrics such as pageviews, bounce rates, and traffic sources, you can make data-driven decisions to improve your SEO strategies and overall user experience. Also, Wix offers built-in analytics that provide detailed reports on your online store's performance, including sales data, customer behavior, and popular products. These insights can help you identify opportunities for growth, optimize your product offerings, and make informed business decisions.

Social Media Integration

Connecting Social Accounts

Social media plays a crucial role in modern marketing and customer engagement. Wix allows you to seamlessly connect your website to various social media platforms, such as Facebook, Instagram, Twitter, and LinkedIn. This integration enables you to showcase your social media presence, share updates, and leverage the power of social media to drive traffic and engagement. By connecting your social accounts, you can embed social feeds directly onto your Wix site, providing visitors with real-time updates and fostering a sense of community around your brand.

Sharing Options

Encourage your visitors to share your content on their social media channels by incorporating sharing buttons on your Wix site. These buttons make it easy for visitors to share your blog posts, products, or other content with their networks, increasing visibility and potential traffic to your website. Wix offers customizable sharing buttons for popular platforms, ensuring a seamless and visually appealing experience for your visitors.

Social Feeds

In addition to connecting your social accounts, Wix allows you to embed social feeds directly onto your website. These feeds display real-time updates, posts, and content from your various social media channels, providing visitors with a dynamic and engaging experience. Social feeds can be customized to match your website's branding and design, ensuring a cohesive look and feel. They can be placed on any page of your Wix site, making it easy for visitors to stay updated with your latest social media activity.

Marketing And Lead Generation

Email Marketing

Email marketing is a powerful tool for nurturing leads, engaging with customers, and driving sales. Wix offers integration with popular email marketing platforms like MailChimp and Constant Contact, allowing you to seamlessly manage your email campaigns from within the Wix platform. Create beautiful email templates that align with your brand's visual identity, segment your email lists based on customer behavior and preferences, and track key metrics like open rates and click-through rates to optimize your campaigns.

Pop-Ups and Forms

Capture visitor information and generate leads with Wix's pop-up and form-building tools. Create customizable pop-ups that appear at strategic times, such as when a visitor lands on your site or attempts to exit, encouraging them to sign up for your newsletter, download a lead magnet, or take advantage of a special offer. Wix also provides a user-friendly form builder that allows you to create contact forms, survey forms, and other lead-capture forms tailored to your specific needs. These forms can be easily embedded on any page of your Wix site, ensuring a seamless user experience.

Retargeting Ads

Retargeting ads are a powerful way to re-engage with visitors who have previously interacted with your website but didn't convert. Wix offers integration with popular retargeting platforms like Google Ads and Facebook Ads, enabling you to display targeted advertisements to these potential customers as they browse the web or social media platforms. By leveraging retargeting ads, you can keep your brand top-of-mind and encourage visitors to return to your website, ultimately increasing conversion rates and driving sales.

Security And Backups

SSL Certificates

Ensuring the security and trust of your website is essential, especially if you're running an online store or handling sensitive customer information. Wix offers built-in SSL (Secure Sockets Layer) certificates, which encrypt data transmissions between your website and visitors' browsers, protecting against potential security breaches and cyber threats. With an SSL certificate, visitors can feel confident that their personal and financial information is secure when interacting with your Wix site, fostering trust and credibility for your brand.

Site Backups

Accidents can happen, and data loss can be devastating for any website or online business. Wix recognizes the importance of safeguarding your hard work by providing automated site backups. These backups ensure that you can quickly restore your website to a previous state in case of any unforeseen issues, such as accidental deletions, hacking attempts, or server failures. With Wix's site backup feature, you can rest assured that your content, data, and site settings are securely stored and easily recoverable, minimizing downtime and potential losses.

Spam Protection

Spam and malicious activities can not only be frustrating but can also harm your website's reputation and security. Wix offers spam protection measures to help safeguard your site from unwanted comments, form submissions, and other potential threats. The platform employs advanced algorithms and filtering techniques to detect and block spam, ensuring that your website remains clean and secure from malicious activities. Additionally, Wix provides tools for moderating comments and form submissions, allowing you to review and approve content before it goes live on your site.

CHAPTER FIVE

PUBLISHING AND
MANAGING YOUR SITE

Domain Registration

Registering a domain is a crucial step in publishing your website. A domain name is the unique address that visitors will use to access your site. When choosing a domain, aim for something memorable, short, and relevant to your brand or website's purpose. Many web hosting providers offer domain registration services, or you can use a dedicated domain registrar. Once you've selected a domain, you'll need to complete the registration process, which typically involves providing personal or business information and paying an annual fee. Be sure to keep your domain registration up-to-date to maintain ownership and avoid potential issues with your website's accessibility.

Web Hosting Options

Web hosting is a service that allows your website files to be stored and accessed on a server connected to the internet. There are various web hosting options available, each with its own set of features and pricing:

1. **Shared Hosting**: This is a cost-effective option where your website shares server resources with other websites. It's suitable for smaller websites with moderate traffic.

2. **Virtual Private Server (VPS) Hosting**: A VPS provides more resources and isolation than shared hosting, making it suitable for websites with higher traffic and resource needs.

3. **Dedicated Server Hosting**: With a dedicated server, you have exclusive access to the server's resources, offering maximum performance and customization options. This is ideal for large, resource-intensive websites.

4. **Cloud Hosting**: Cloud hosting utilizes a network of servers to distribute your website's resources, providing scalability and redundancy.

When selecting a web hosting plan, consider factors such as disk space, bandwidth, uptime guarantees, security features, and customer support. Many hosting providers offer different tiers of services to accommodate varying website needs and budgets.

Launching Your Website

Once you've registered your domain and secured web hosting, you're ready to launch your website. This process typically involves uploading your website files to the hosting server and configuring the domain to point to your hosting account.

Before launching, it's essential to thoroughly test your website across different devices and browsers to ensure a consistent user experience. Additionally, you'll want to optimize your website for search engines by implementing best practices for on-page SEO, such as optimizing titles, meta descriptions, and header tags.

Site Maintenance And Updates

Maintaining your website is an ongoing process that involves regularly updating content, plugins, and software to ensure optimal performance and security. Neglecting updates can leave your website vulnerable to security breaches, compatibility issues, and a degraded user experience.

Set a schedule for backing up your website files and database regularly, as well as updating any content management systems (CMS), plugins, or themes you're using. Stay informed about any security vulnerabilities or software updates that may affect your website, and promptly address them.

Analyzing Website Traffic

Understanding your website's traffic patterns is crucial for making informed decisions about content, marketing strategies, and website optimization. Various web analytics tools, such as Google Analytics, provide valuable insights into your website's traffic sources, visitor behavior, and demographic data. Regularly analyzing your website's traffic data can help you identify popular content, pinpoint areas for improvement, and track the effectiveness of your marketing efforts. Use this information to refine your content strategy, optimize your website's user experience, and make data-driven decisions to improve your online presence.

Troubleshooting Common Issues

Despite your best efforts, website issues may arise from time to time. Common problems can include broken links, slow page load times, server errors, and compatibility issues with certain browsers or devices. Develop a troubleshooting process to identify and resolve these issues promptly. This may involve checking server logs, testing your website across different environments, and seeking assistance from your web hosting provider or developer community forums.

A continuous monitoring of your website's performance and addressing any issues proactively can help minimize downtime and ensure a seamless user experience for your visitors.

Getting Help And Support

Building and managing a website can be a complex task, especially for those new to the process. Fortunately, there are various resources available to assist you, such as:

1. **Documentation and Knowledge Bases**: Many web hosting providers, content management systems, and web development platforms offer comprehensive documentation, tutorials, and knowledge bases to help you navigate their services and features.

2. **Community Forums**: Engaging with online communities dedicated to web development and website management can provide valuable insights, troubleshooting tips, and best practices from experienced users and professionals.

3. **Professional Services**: If you encounter issues beyond your expertise or have limited time, consider hiring a professional web developer or agency to assist with specific tasks or provide ongoing website maintenance and support.

Don't hesitate to seek help when needed. Leveraging the right resources and support can save you time, frustration, and ensure your website operates smoothly and effectively.

CHAPTER SIX

ADVANCED DESIGN TECHNIQUES

Using Wix Animations

Animations can add a dynamic and engaging touch to your website, guiding visitors' attention and enhancing the overall user experience. Wix offers a range of animation options to bring your content to life.

Entrance Animations Entrance animations are triggered when an element appears on the screen, creating a smooth and visually appealing transition. These animations can be applied to text, images, or entire sections, instantly grabbing your visitors' attention. From fading in to sliding or bouncing effects, entrance animations can be customized to suit your brand and design aesthetic.

Scroll Animations Scroll animations are triggered as visitors scroll through your website, adding a sense of movement and keeping them engaged. These animations can be used to reveal content progressively, highlight key sections, or create parallax effects for a depth-like experience. Wix's intuitive animation builder allows you to fine-tune the timing, duration, and behavior of scroll animations, ensuring a seamless and captivating user journey.

Hover Effects Hover effects are triggered when visitors hover over an element, such as a button, image, or text. These effects can add interactivity and visual interest, encouraging visitors to explore and engage with your content further. From subtle scale changes to innovative hover animations, Wix's hover effects can elevate the overall user experience and enhance your website's professional appeal.

Creating Custom Layouts

Wix offers a powerful layout system that allows you to create unique and visually striking designs tailored to your specific needs.

Working with Strips Strips are horizontal sections that span the width of your website. They serve as building blocks for creating custom layouts, allowing you to combine various elements such as text, images, and multimedia. With Wix's drag-and-drop interface, you can easily arrange and adjust strips to achieve your desired layout.

Using Grids and Sections Grids and sections provide a structured approach to organizing your content within strips. Grids allow you to divide your page into columns and rows, ensuring a consistent and visually appealing layout. Sections, on the other hand, act as containers for specific content, enabling you to group related elements together and control their appearance and behavior.

Responsive Design Techniques With the increasing use of mobile devices, it's crucial to ensure your website looks great and functions seamlessly across various screen sizes. Wix's responsive design tools allow you to optimize your layouts for different devices, ensuring a consistent and user-friendly experience. You can adjust element sizes, spacing, and visibility, as well as implement mobile-specific designs, ensuring your website adapts seamlessly to any screen size.

Building Interactive Elements

Interactive elements encourage visitor engagement and can enhance the overall user experience on your website.

Forms and Surveys Forms and surveys are powerful tools for collecting data from your visitors. Wix offers a wide range of form templates and customization options, allowing you to gather valuable information such as contact details, feedback, or survey responses. With built-in form validation and submission tracking, you can ensure a smooth and efficient data collection process.

Calculators and Quizzes Calculators and quizzes can be valuable additions to your website, providing visitors with interactive tools that enhance their understanding or assist them in making informed decisions. Wix's calculator and quiz builders make it easy to create custom calculators, quizzes, and assessments, complete with scoring mechanisms and result displays.

Appointment Booking If your business offers services that require appointments, Wix's appointment booking feature can streamline the scheduling process. Visitors can conveniently book appointments directly through your website, reducing administrative overhead and ensuring a seamless experience for both you and your customers.

Leveraging Wix Code

While Wix's intuitive interface and built-in features cater to most website needs, there may be instances where you require more advanced functionality. This is where Wix Code comes into play.

Introduction to Wix Code Wix Code is a powerful tool that allows you to extend the capabilities of your website using JavaScript and Web Development APIs. With Wix Code, you can create custom interactions, automate processes, and integrate with third-party services, unlocking a world of possibilities for your website.

Customizing Site Behavior Using Wix Code, you can

customize various aspects of your website's behavior, such as implementing complex form validations, creating dynamic content updates, or implementing custom navigation menus. By leveraging JavaScript's flexibility, you can tailor your website's functionality to meet your specific requirements.

Integrating Third-Party APIs Wix Code also enables you to integrate with third-party APIs, allowing you to leverage external services and data sources. Whether you want to incorporate social media feeds, payment gateways, or analytics tools, Wix Code provides the framework to seamlessly integrate these services into your website, enhancing its functionality and capabilities.

With these advanced design techniques, you can create websites that stand out, engage visitors, and provide a truly immersive and professional experience. Whether you're a seasoned designer or just starting out, Wix's powerful tools and features empower you to bring your vision to life.

CHAPTER SEVEN

*CONTENT MANAGEMENT
AND BLOGGING*

Setting Up A Blog

Blogging is a powerful way to engage with your audience, share your expertise, and drive traffic to your website. Wix provides a user-friendly blogging platform that allows you to create and manage a professional-looking blog seamlessly integrated with your website.

Creating Blog Posts

To create a new blog post, navigate to the Blog Manager and click "Create a New Post." The rich text editor lets you format your content with ease, adding headings, lists, images, and videos. You can also schedule your posts for future publication or save drafts for later revision.

Blog Layout And Design

Wix offers a variety of customizable blog templates to

match the branding and style of your website. You can choose from different layout options, such as a classic blog roll, grid view, or masonry layout. Customize the fonts, colors, and other design elements to create a cohesive and visually appealing blog.

Categories And Tags

Organize your blog posts by assigning categories and tags. Categories allow you to group related posts together, while tags help visitors find specific topics they're interested in. This not only enhances the user experience but also improves your blog's SEO visibility.

Working With Content Management

Wix's intuitive content management system empowers you to create, organize, and publish various types of content beyond blog posts, such as articles, news updates, or resource libraries.

Creating Content Libraries

Build content libraries to store and manage your files, images, videos, and other digital assets in one centralized location. This streamlines the process of adding rich media to your website or blog posts, ensuring consistency and easy access to your content.

Managing And Organizing Content

Within the Content Manager, you can create folders and subfolders to organize your content in a logical hierarchy. This makes it easier to find and reuse existing content, saving you time and effort in the long run.

Scheduling Content Updates

Stay in control of your content calendar by scheduling updates in advance. Whether it's publishing a new blog post, updating an existing page, or promoting a special offer, you can plan and schedule your content to go live at the most opportune times.

Optimizing Content For Seo

Effective content optimization is crucial for improving your website's visibility and attracting organic traffic from search engines.

Keyword Research

Identify relevant keywords and phrases that your target audience is searching for. Use tools like Google's Keyword

ANDREW G. WILLARD

Planner or SEMrush to research high-volume, low-competition keywords to incorporate into your content.

On-Page Optimization

Optimize your content for search engines by incorporating keywords strategically into your headings, body text, meta descriptions, and image alt text. Ensure your content is well-structured, easy to read, and provides value to your visitors.

Sitemaps And Structured Data

Submit an XML sitemap to search engines to help them crawl and index your website's content more efficiently. Additionally, implement structured data markup to provide search engines with rich, contextual information about your content, potentially enhancing your search visibility and click-through rates.

Remember, creating high-quality, engaging content is key to building a loyal audience and achieving your website's goals. Wix's comprehensive content management and blogging tools empower you to create, organize, and optimize your content effectively, while maintaining a professional and visually appealing online presence.

CHAPTER EIGHT

*ANALYTICS AND CONVERSION
OPTIMIZATION*

Understanding Website Analytics

Website analytics provide valuable insights into user behavior, enabling website owners to make data-driven decisions and optimize their online presence. By analyzing key metrics, businesses can gain a comprehensive understanding of their audience, identify areas for improvement, and ultimately enhance their overall performance.

Visitor Metrics

Visitor metrics offer a glimpse into the demographics and characteristics of the individuals accessing your website. These metrics include:

- **User Demographics:** Gain insights into the age, gender, and geographic location of your visitors, allowing you to tailor your content and marketing efforts accordingly.

- **New vs. Returning Visitors:** Understand the ratio of new and returning visitors, which can help assess the effectiveness of your acquisition and retention strategies.
- **Device Usage:** Analyze the devices (desktop, mobile, tablet) used by your visitors to access your website, ensuring that your site is optimized for various screen sizes and platforms.
- **Visit Duration:** Monitor the average time visitors spend on your website, indicating the level of engagement and interest in your content.

Traffic Sources

Understanding where your website traffic originates is crucial for optimizing your marketing efforts and allocating resources effectively. Traffic sources can include:

- **Organic Search:** Monitor the volume of visitors coming from search engines like Google and Bing, and identify the keywords driving the most traffic.
- **Referral Traffic:** Track the websites and platforms that are referring visitors to your site, allowing you to cultivate relationships with valuable referral sources.
- **Direct Traffic:** Analyze the number of visitors who directly access your website by typing the URL or using bookmarks, indicating brand awareness and loyalty.
- **Social Media:** Evaluate the effectiveness of your social media presence by tracking the traffic generated from various platforms like Facebook, Twitter, and LinkedIn.

Behavior Analysis

Behavior analysis provides insights into how users interact with your website, enabling you to identify potential friction points and areas for improvement:

- **Page Views:** Monitor the most frequently visited pages on your website, indicating the content that resonates with your audience.
- **Bounce Rate:** Analyze the percentage of visitors who leave your site after viewing a single page, which can highlight issues with content quality or user experience.
- **Navigation Patterns:** Understand the paths users take through your website, revealing opportunities to optimize the flow and structure of your site.
- **Event Tracking:** Track specific user interactions, such as clicks, form submissions, or video plays, to measure engagement and conversion rates.

Tracking Conversions

Conversions represent the desired actions you want visitors to take on your website, such as making a purchase, filling out a form, or subscribing to a newsletter. Effective conversion tracking is essential for evaluating the success of your website and marketing efforts.

Defining Conversion Goals

The first step in tracking conversions is to define your conversion goals clearly. These goals should align with your business objectives and may include:

- **E-commerce Transactions:** Track completed purchases, revenue generated, and average order value.
- **Lead Generation:** Monitor form submissions, newsletter signups, or contact requests.
- **Content Engagement:** Measure interactions with your content, such as downloads, video views, or social shares.
- **Subscription Signups:** Track new subscription acquisitions for your products or services.

Setting Up Conversion Tracking

Once your conversion goals are defined, you can set up conversion tracking within your analytics platform. This typically involves:

- **Event Tracking:** Implementing code snippets or triggers to track specific user actions on your website.
- **Goal Configuration:** Creating conversion goals within your analytics platform and assigning them to the relevant events or page visits.
- **Funnel Visualization:** Visualizing the conversion funnel to identify drop-off points and optimize the user journey.

A/B Testing

A/B testing, also known as split testing, is a powerful technique for optimizing conversions. It involves creating multiple versions of a web page or element and presenting them to different segments of your audience. By analyzing the performance of each variation, you can determine which version drives higher conversion rates and make data-driven decisions for improvement.

User Experience Optimization

Enhancing the user experience on your website is crucial for driving conversions and fostering customer satisfaction. A seamless and engaging experience can lead to increased engagement, loyalty, and ultimately, conversions.

Heatmaps And Session Recordings

Heatmaps and session recordings provide valuable insights into how users interact with your website. Heatmaps visually represent areas of a web page that receive the most attention and clicks, while session recordings capture visitors' mouse movements, clicks, and scrolling behavior. By analyzing these data sources, you can identify areas of friction, optimize page layouts, and streamline user flows.

Improving Site Speed

Site speed is a critical factor in the user experience. Slow-loading pages can lead to high bounce rates and decreased conversions. To improve site speed, consider:

- **Image Optimization:** Compress and resize images to reduce file sizes without compromising quality.
- **Leveraging Caching:** Implement caching mechanisms to serve static content more efficiently.
- **Minimizing HTTP Requests:** Combine and minify CSS and JavaScript files to reduce the number of requests made to the server.
- **Content Delivery Networks (CDNs):** Utilize CDNs to distribute content from servers closest to the user, reducing latency.

Enhancing User Interactions

Providing a seamless and intuitive user experience can significantly impact conversions. Consider the following strategies:

- **Responsive Design:** Ensure your website is optimized for various devices and screen sizes, providing a consistent experience across platforms.
- **Simplified Navigation:** Implement clear and intuitive navigation menus, making it easy for users to find the information they need.
- **Reduce Friction:** Streamline form fields, checkout processes, and other user interactions to

minimize friction and increase conversion rates.

- **Incorporate Visual Cues:** Use visual cues, such as directional arrows or highlights, to guide users through the desired actions and conversion paths.

By continuously analyzing and optimizing these aspects of your website, you can enhance the user experience, increase conversions, and drive better business outcomes.

CHAPTER NINE

MARKETING AND PROMOTION

Email Marketing Strategies

Building Email Lists Developing a strong email list is crucial for effective email marketing campaigns. Start by offering value to your target audience, such as a free e-book, a webinar, or exclusive content in exchange for their email addresses. Make sure to have a prominent opt-in form on your website's homepage and other high-traffic pages. Additionally, consider offering incentives like discounts or giveaways to encourage visitors to subscribe. Leverage your existing customer base by including an opt-in option during the checkout process or by inviting them to join your email list. Remember to comply with anti-spam laws and provide a clear option for subscribers to unsubscribe.

Creating Newsletters Engaging newsletters are the backbone of successful email marketing campaigns. Craft compelling subject lines that grab attention and entice recipients to open your emails. Provide valuable, relevant content that resonates with your audience, such as industry news, tips, and exclusive offers. Use a consistent branding and design to reinforce your brand identity. Segment your email list based on interests, demographics, or behavior to deliver personalized content that resonates better with each group. Include clear calls-to-action that guide subscribers to take the desired action, whether it's making a purchase, visiting your website, or sharing your content on social media.

Email Automation Automating your email campaigns can significantly improve efficiency and deliver timely, relevant messages to your subscribers. Set up welcome emails to greet new subscribers and introduce them to your brand. Create nurture sequences that provide valuable information and gradually guide prospects through the sales funnel. Implement abandoned cart emails to remind shoppers about items left in their cart and encourage them to complete the purchase. Leverage customer data to send personalized product recommendations, birthday greetings, or re-engagement campaigns for inactive subscribers. Automate your email marketing efforts to save time and deliver a seamless customer experience.

Social Media Marketing

Social Media Platforms Identify the social media platforms where your target audience is most active and establish a strong presence there. Popular platforms like

Facebook, Instagram, Twitter, LinkedIn, and YouTube offer unique opportunities to connect with your audience, share valuable content, and promote your products or services. Tailor your content strategy to each platform's strengths, such as visuals for Instagram, short updates for Twitter, and longer-form content for LinkedIn. Engage with your followers by responding to comments, asking questions, and encouraging user-generated content.

Content Promotion Develop a content promotion strategy to maximize the reach and visibility of your social media posts. Share a mix of original content, curated content from trusted sources, and promotional updates. Use compelling visuals, such as images, videos, or infographics, to capture attention and increase engagement. Leverage social media advertising options to boost your most valuable content and reach a broader audience. Encourage your existing followers to share your content with their networks by running contests, offering incentives, or creating shareable, viral-worthy content.

Paid Advertising While organic social media efforts are essential, paid advertising can significantly amplify your reach and drive targeted traffic to your website or landing pages. Platforms like Facebook, Instagram, and LinkedIn offer advanced targeting options to reach specific demographics, interests, behaviors, and even custom audiences. Experiment with different ad formats, such as single image ads, carousel ads, or video ads, to find what resonates best with your audience. Continuously monitor and optimize your ad campaigns based on performance metrics, adjusting targeting, ad creative, and budgets as needed.

Search Engine Marketing (Sem)

Pay-Per-Click Advertising Pay-per-click (PPC) advertising is a powerful tool for driving targeted traffic to your website. Platforms like Google Ads and Bing Ads allow you to create text-based or display ads that appear when users search for specific keywords or browse relevant websites. Conduct thorough keyword research to identify the most relevant and profitable keywords for your business. Craft compelling ad copy that resonates with your target audience and encourages them to click. Set up targeted ad campaigns based on geographic location, device type, and other factors to ensure your ads reach the right audience.

Keyword Research and Targeting Effective keyword research is crucial for both organic search engine optimization (SEO) and paid search engine marketing (SEM) efforts. Use tools like Google Keyword Planner, SEMrush, or Ahrefs to identify relevant keywords with high search volume and moderate competition. Consider long-tail keywords that are more specific and targeted to your products or services. Analyze your competitors' keyword strategies to identify gaps and opportunities. Incorporate your target keywords strategically into your website content, meta tags, and ad campaigns for maximum visibility and relevance.

Campaign Management Managing your search engine marketing campaigns effectively is essential for achieving optimal results and maximizing your return on investment (ROI). Set clear campaign goals, whether it's driving website traffic, generating leads, or increasing sales. Continuously monitor key performance indicators (KPIs) such as click-through rates, conversion rates, and cost-per-acquisition to assess the success of your campaigns. Use A/B testing to experiment with different ad copy, landing pages, and targeting options to identify the most effective strategies. Regularly adjust your bids, budgets, and targeting based on performance data to optimize your campaigns for maximum efficiency and profitability.

CHAPTER TEN

GOING BEYOND WIX

Integrating With Third-Party Tools

As your business grows, you may find the need to integrate your Wix website with other third-party tools and software to streamline your operations and enhance functionality. Wix offers integration capabilities with various popular platforms, allowing you to seamlessly connect your website with essential business tools.

CRM Systems Customer Relationship Management (CRM) systems are crucial for managing customer interactions, sales pipelines, and lead nurturing. By integrating your Wix website with a CRM system like Salesforce, HubSpot, or Zoho, you can capture lead information from online forms, automate data synchronization, and streamline your sales and marketing processes. This integration ensures that valuable customer data is centralized, allowing you to provide personalized experiences and improve customer retention.

Accounting Software Integrating your Wix website with

accounting software like QuickBooks or Xero can simplify your financial management tasks. This integration enables you to automatically sync online orders, invoices, and payment information, reducing manual data entry and minimizing errors. With real-time financial data at your fingertips, you can make informed business decisions and maintain accurate financial records.

Project Management Tools For businesses that collaborate on projects or manage client work, integrating Wix with project management tools like Trello, Asana, or Jira can significantly enhance productivity and organization. These integrations allow you to create tasks, assign responsibilities, and track progress directly from your website, ensuring seamless communication and efficient project execution.

Expanding With Web Apps

As your business grows and requirements evolve, you may need to extend the functionality of your Wix website beyond its built-in capabilities. Wix offers the ability to integrate with web apps, opening up a world of possibilities for customization and advanced features.

Web App Development Wix provides a platform for developing custom web apps using their proprietary technology, Velo. With Velo, developers can build interactive, data-driven applications that integrate seamlessly with your Wix website. These web apps can range from simple tools to complex business applications, tailored to your specific needs.

Integrating Web Apps with Wix Once you have developed or acquired a web app, you can easily integrate it with your Wix website. This integration allows you to embed the web app directly into your website's pages, providing a cohesive user experience. Web apps can be used for various purposes, such as e-commerce solutions, appointment booking systems, learning management platforms, or any custom functionality you require.

Exploring Wix Code Advanced Features

For businesses and developers looking to push the boundaries of what's possible with Wix, the Wix Code platform offers advanced features and capabilities for building sophisticated, data-driven applications.

Custom Database Integrations Wix Code allows you to connect your website to external databases, such as MySQL, PostgreSQL, or MongoDB. This integration enables you to store and retrieve data from these databases, facilitating the creation of dynamic, data-driven applications. Whether you need to manage inventory, user profiles, or any other type of data, custom database integrations provide the flexibility and scalability you need.

Building Dynamic Applications With Wix Code, you

can create dynamic web applications that respond to user interactions and data changes in real-time. Leverage powerful programming capabilities to build complex logic, implement custom algorithms, and create interactive user interfaces. This opens up a world of possibilities for developing unique and engaging applications tailored to your business needs.

Deploying to Custom Domains While Wix provides a subdomain for hosting your website, you may want to deploy your application to a custom domain or even a dedicated server for enhanced performance and customization. Wix Code supports deployment to custom domains, allowing you to host your application on your own domain or a third-party hosting service, providing greater control and branding opportunities.

By leveraging the advanced features of Wix Code, you can transform your Wix website into a fully-fledged web application, pushing the boundaries of functionality and delivering a truly unique and tailored experience for your users.

CHAPTER ELEVEN

RESOURCES AND BEST
PRACTICES

Wix App Market And Extensions

The Wix App Market is a vast collection of third-party applications, tools, and extensions designed to enhance your website's functionality and user experience. These apps are developed by Wix's partners and the Wix community, offering a wide range of features and capabilities to cater to various business needs. One of the primary advantages of the Wix App Market is its ease of integration. With just a few clicks, you can seamlessly install and incorporate these apps into your Wix website, without the need for any complex coding or technical expertise. This empowers you to customize and tailor your website to meet your specific requirements, regardless of your technical background.

Some popular app categories in the Wix App Market include:

1. **E-commerce Solutions**: Enable online sales,

manage inventory, process payments, and streamline your online store with robust e-commerce apps.

2. **Marketing and Promotional Tools**: Engage your audience, run targeted campaigns, and analyze website performance with apps focused on marketing, analytics, and lead generation.

3. **Communication and Collaboration**: Enhance communication and collaboration with apps for live chat, appointment scheduling, and integrating popular productivity tools like Google Workspace or Microsoft Office.

4. **Social Media Integration**: Connect your website to various social media platforms, enabling easy sharing, displaying social feeds, and leveraging the power of social media for your business.

5. **Media and Content Management**: Enhance your website's multimedia capabilities with apps for video galleries, photo sliders, and content management systems.

6. **Website Optimization**: Improve website performance, security, and user experience with apps for caching, minification, and accessibility enhancements.

Wix continuously updates and expands the App Market, allowing you to stay up-to-date with the latest trends and technologies. By leveraging these powerful extensions, you can create a dynamic, feature-rich website tailored to your specific needs, without sacrificing the ease of use and flexibility that Wix is known for.

Common Pitfalls To Avoid

While Wix provides a user-friendly platform for building websites, there are certain pitfalls and challenges that users should be aware of to ensure a smooth and successful website creation process. Here are some common pitfalls to avoid:

1. **Neglecting Mobile Responsiveness**: With the majority of internet users accessing websites from mobile devices, it's crucial to ensure that your website is fully responsive and optimized for various screen sizes and resolutions. Neglecting mobile responsiveness can lead to a poor user experience, increased bounce rates, and potential loss of customers or visitors.

2. **Overreliance on Templates**: While Wix offers a vast selection of pre-designed templates, it's essential to customize and personalize them to create a unique and distinct website. Overreliance on templates without proper customization can result in a generic, cookie-cutter website that fails to stand out from the competition.

3. **Lack of SEO Optimization**: Search engine optimization (SEO) is vital for ensuring that your website is visible and easily discoverable on search engines. Neglecting SEO best practices, such as optimizing meta tags, content structure, and site speed, can significantly limit your website's online visibility and organic traffic.

4. **Ignoring Content Management**: Content is

the backbone of any successful website. Failing to plan and implement a robust content management strategy can lead to outdated, irrelevant, or disorganized information, negatively impacting the user experience and your website's credibility.

5. **Overlooking Site Security**: Website security should be a top priority, especially if you handle sensitive data or conduct online transactions. Neglecting security measures, such as SSL certificates, secure payment gateways, and regular software updates, can expose your website and its visitors to potential cyber threats.

6. **Excessive Use of Third-Party Apps**: While Wix's App Market offers a wealth of useful extensions, excessive reliance on third-party apps can lead to compatibility issues, performance bottlenecks, and potential security vulnerabilities. It's essential to strike a balance and carefully evaluate the necessity and reliability of each app before integrating it into your website.

By being aware of these common pitfalls and adopting best practices, you can create a professional, user-friendly, and successful website on the Wix platform, while avoiding unnecessary challenges and roadblocks.

Future Trends And Emerging Technologies

The world of web development and online presence is constantly evolving, driven by advancements in technology, changing user behaviors, and emerging trends.

As a Wix user, it's essential to stay informed about these trends and emerging technologies to ensure that your website remains relevant, competitive, and aligned with the latest industry standards. Here are some future trends and emerging technologies to watch out for:

1. **Artificial Intelligence and Machine Learning**: AI and machine learning are transforming various aspects of the web development process, from content creation and personalization to user experience optimization and predictive analytics. Wix may incorporate these technologies to offer intelligent website building tools, automated content generation, and personalized user experiences based on user behavior and preferences.

2. **Voice Search and Conversational Interfaces**: With the increasing popularity of virtual assistants and voice-controlled devices, voice search and conversational interfaces are becoming more prevalent. Websites may need to adapt their content and structure to cater to voice search queries and integrate conversational interfaces to enhance user engagement and accessibility.

3. **Augmented Reality (AR) and Virtual Reality (VR)**: As immersive technologies like AR and VR continue to evolve, they may find applications in various industries, including e-commerce, real estate, and tourism. Wix may introduce features or integrations that allow businesses to showcase their products or services through AR or VR

experiences, enhancing customer engagement and providing a unique competitive advantage.

4. **Progressive Web Apps (PWAs)**: PWAs are web applications that combine the best features of traditional websites and mobile apps, offering a seamless, app-like experience across various devices and platforms. Wix may explore PWA development to provide users with the ability to create responsive, fast-loading, and offline-capable websites that can be installed on users' devices like native apps.

5. **Internet of Things (IoT) and Connected Devices**: As the Internet of Things continues to expand, with more devices and appliances becoming connected, there may be opportunities for Wix to integrate IoT functionality into websites, enabling businesses to control and monitor connected devices, collect data, and automate processes.

6. **Blockchain and Decentralized Web**: While still in its early stages, the decentralized web and blockchain technology have the potential to revolutionize various aspects of the online world, including data security, privacy, and transparency. Wix may explore ways to leverage these technologies to enhance website security, enable decentralized content management, or facilitate secure transactions.

7. **Sustainable Web Design**: With increasing awareness of environmental issues, sustainable web design practices are gaining traction. This includes optimizing websites for energy

efficiency, reducing carbon footprints, and promoting eco-friendly practices in web development and hosting.

By staying informed about these trends and emerging technologies, you can position your Wix website for long-term success, adapting to changing user expectations and leveraging the latest advancements to provide an exceptional online experience for your visitors and customers.

CONCLUSION

Summarily, beyond its enormous collection of apps and templates, Wix is setting the standard for security, accessibility, performance, dependability, and analytics. In this guide has explored the vast capabilities of Wix, a powerful website creation platform designed for users of all skill levels. From setting up your account and navigating the intuitive interface to crafting visually stunning pages and leveraging advanced features, we have covered a wide range of topics to equip you with the knowledge and tools necessary to build a professional-grade website.

Let us briefly recap the key aspects we've discussed:

1. **Getting Started with Wix**: We walked through the process of signing up for a Wix account and familiarized ourselves with the user-friendly interface. This initial step paved the way for a smooth and enjoyable website-building experience.

2. **Creating a New Website**: We delved into the process of creating a new website from scratch, exploring the various templates and design options available. We learned how to customize

these templates to align with your brand's unique identity and messaging.

3. **Adding Design Elements**: One of Wix's strengths lies in its extensive design capabilities. We explored how to incorporate various design elements, such as images, videos, text, and shapes, to enhance the visual appeal and functionality of your website.

4. **Building Pages**: We covered the art of crafting individual pages for your website, including techniques for organizing content, structuring layouts, and ensuring a seamless user experience across different page types.

5. **Advanced Features**: To take your website to the next level, we explored advanced features like e-commerce integration, blogging tools, and third-party app integration. These powerful tools enable you to create a comprehensive online presence tailored to your specific needs.

6. **Tools and Settings**: We discussed the various tools and settings available in Wix, empowering you to fine-tune your website's performance, optimize search engine visibility, and manage user interactions effectively.

7. **Publishing Your Website**: Finally, we guided you through the process of publishing your website, making it live and accessible to the world. We also covered essential post-publication maintenance tasks to ensure your website remains up-to-date and engaging.

In conclusion. as you embark on your journey with Wix,

remember that practice and experimentation are key to mastering this versatile platform. Don't be afraid to explore different design options, experiment with new features, and continuously refine your website to better serve your target audience. Embrace the power of Wix, unleash your creativity, and embark on an exciting journey to build a website that truly represents your vision and leaves a lasting impression on your visitors. The possibilities are endless, and the path to success lies within your grasp.